Susan!
Let poetry be the
light we see by—and
let the heart
be a lantern.
Jim

imagination series #7

ACKNOWLEDGMENTS

I would like to acknowledge the following publications in which several of these
poems were featured:

Callaloo: "Hey Man"
Controlled Burn: "Bell Street Blues"
The Cape Cod Voice: "Fearless," "Harvest Moon"
Electronic Poetry Review: "Bell Street Blues," "Playing Catch"
Flyway: "First Kiss," "Ambition: Mosquito in the Mist"
Harper's Ferry: "Welcome Home"
HEArt: "Really Breathing"
Indiana Review: "Further"
Kente Cloth: *"Wha'chu Shoulda* // Told the Brother"
The Literary Review: "Bonobo"
New Letters: "At 41," "Christmas 2001," "Cow & Microphone," "First Verse"
(under the title "Mercy"), "Lobster For Sale," and "Spoken"
North American Review: "Night Flight"
The Progressive: "Not Spoken"
Rattle: "Late Shift"
64: "Meditations from a Small Plane in Bad Weather"

———

Dark Eros (anthology): "Someone Else" (under the title "A Bit More")
Role Call (anthology): "Back," "Invasion of the Body Snatchers," "The Further
    Adventures of Tutor the Turtle"

———

I would also like to thank Mille Grazie Press for the publication of the chapbook
Ten Miles An Hour in which "Invasion of the Body Snatchers," "Renegades," and
"Will Not Be Televised" first appeared. And special thanks to the editors of *The
Blue Collar Review* for their hard work and support.

Published by Cleveland State University Poetry Center
2121 Euclid Avenue
Cleveland, OH 44115-2214

ISBN: 1-880834-63-4 (paper)
ISBN: 1-880834-64-2 (cloth)

Library of Congress Catalog
Card Number: 20033111521

Ohio Arts Council
A STATE AGENCY
THAT SUPPORTS PUBLIC
PROGRAMS IN THE ARTS

Buffalo Head Solos

poems by Tim Seibles

Cleveland State University Poetry Center

Buffalo Head Solos

Contents

for June Jordan and Pablo Neruda

I believe in the great day
Which will make our paths meet:
I shall wake then from the desert
Seeing you approach with pots filled with water.

– Mazisi Kunene
from *Zulu Poems*

An Open Letter

I want to talk about some of the things I'm after when I write, my sense of the American predicament, and what I hope for poetry and for people in relation to words. I know I'm also talking to myself here, and I can't speak to the success or failure of what transpires in the poems that follow. I simply hope that this short rant can provide a clarifying context, a brief look at what confounds and compels my efforts. I realize, of course, that this could be bone-headedly presumptuous, but there are things far worse than speaking out of turn.

In fact, part of what energizes me is all the nay-saying I hear about what poets and poetry can do: *Poetry will never reach the general public. Poetry shouldn't be political or argumentative. Poetry will not succeed if it's excessively imaginative. Poetry can't change anything.* Because the first people I heard saying such things were poets, I used to believe these notions were born of thoughtful consideration and humility, but now I see them as a kind of preemptive apology, a small-hearted justification for the writing of a hobbled poetry – a poetry that doesn't want to be too conspicuous, a poetry that knows its place, that doesn't mean to trouble the water, that is always decorous and never stomps in with bad breath and plaid boots.

But *why not?* Why not a sublimely reckless poetry – when the ascendant social order permits nearly every type of corruption and related hypocrisy? Why not risk more and more? So much is at stake. This culture, deranged by both spoken and unspoken imperatives, mocks the complexity of our loneliness, our spiritual hunger for dynamic meanings, our thirst for genuine human community, for good magic and good sense. And, given the growing heap of human wreckage, why not approach language and its transforming potential with a ravishing hunger, with a ferocity bordering on the psychotic? What the hell happened to the notion of poet as town crier, rabble rouser, court jester, priestess, visionary, madman? Given the way things have gone, it's almost impossible not to be overtaken by despair. Writing poems in SUV-America can feel like fiddling amidst catastrophe, but if one must fiddle shouldn't one play that thing till it smokes? And in stirring the words with our tongues, our paws, our long nights, and the smoldering tangle of our brains, maybe we could move our general kin to listen.

The mainstream discourse is dominated by pop *muzak*, murderously repetitive police dramas, spineless newscasts, insipid movies, and simple-minded talk-shows. Even if we, as poets, do find ourselves regularly locked in the attic, we assist in our own erasure if we accept this gag without a fight. Shoving poetry – and Art in general – to the margins is simply a way to diminish the necessity of paying sincere and unpredictable kinds of attention. I have grown sick to death of meeting people who say they don't *like* poetry, can't *understand* poetry, when they probably haven't read any since high school when they were offered a few leaden standards whose anemic music was further muted by a number of teachers who taught the poems lovelessly in a "unit," then gave a test. This dim view of poetry and contemplation has spread like a flu (and now we have a society so accustomed to semi-literate buffoonery that many of us find it acceptable in those who hold even the highest offices).

Why act as if this were *just the way it is*, as if there were little we – as poets – could do to renovate the house of living words. Maybe we could measure more critically the distance that separates us from, say, a *non*-academic audience. Maybe we can speak more irresistibly, more often, and to more people, unless the prevailing lack of essential speech has so defeated us that we've simply decided to die earnestly at our desks. I can't believe this is the case, and I can't stop thinking that good poems – in a kind of chorus on the loose – *could* comprise a general invitation to a much needed wakefulness.

A lot of people are starving for better light to see by, searching as they are in the well-worn shadows. At the very least, poetry could be one tasty dish in a much needed feast: we should serenade those who don't know poems, who fear poems, who don't trust words that ask them to step into new sensations and unsanctioned territories. We should pursue them as though we are love-struck and cannot help it. I'm only half-kidding. How else can people enlarge their grasp of what being alive means? And why else are we here? The alternative – stoically scratching our heads while the world burns down – is simply too degrading to the helpful purpose of language and to *our lives* as people who work to illuminate the possibilities of consciousness.

I think about being *in America*, being a citizen and poet living in the American Empire, home of truly virulent strains of racism, sexism, *money*ism – and now, a wildly aggressive nationalism which may force us to live with war and its omnivorous machinery for far longer than the Bush Regime holds sway. Why write as if the socio-political atmosphere doesn't have direct bearing on how everyone makes it through each day? (The fact that black people, for instance, die disproportionately of hypertension and other stress-related ailments is *not* a coincidence.) Isn't bad news a kind of weather, a surging storm we lean into every time we open our eyes? The intricacies of our various travels between optimism and cynicism are utterly shaped by the society we inhabit – and the delight or rage each of us lives with hour by hour defines our style of travel, the tenor of our lives. The growing presence of *the dumb-ass zombie* must be a sign that, for many, it's simply better to be deaf and blind than to respond to the world that surrounds us.

Doesn't a working *Democracy* require a full-hearted willingness to voice everything, to insist upon a chance for the most hopeful outcomes? Isn't the current prevalence of smiling apathy and timid speech an emblem of a whelming fascism? Whether this is driven by Big Business, The State, The Church, or all of these in concert doesn't matter. I don't want to be a member of a society famous for its massive yet poorly distributed wealth, its high-tech fire-power, its environmental stupidity, and its somnambulant, sports-loving population. And, if I must be a citizen in such a place, I certainly don't want my poems to be in cahoots with the nightmare. Why should poems merely add mild spice to a cultural medley that affirms a plague of perpetual consumption and really loud cheering?

I believe poetry can be proof that dynamic awareness is alive and kicking, a constant reminder to ourselves and to our fellow citizens that being alert, both inwardly and outwardly, rewards each person with *more* life. Doesn't a good poem bring that electric sense of things, that edgy vitality that can't be laughed off or shopped away? I think being fully human demands this, demands *poetry*.

I say let the poems move in all ways; at least, then, we'll have a chance to reach the bridge – and if we *do* lose our minds let it be because we believed too much in the heart's voice. Where else will we find the most cataclysmic wing of the imagination revealed in words? The dim-witted drowsiness that remains so pervasive is proof of the gradual asphyxiation of the sweetest human yearnings, a kind of spiritual anorexia. Consider how much of our story we've already conceded to Science and its efficient *objectivism*. Consider how the big religions seal our lips and drive the herd with that locked-down, self-perpetuating, *God-says-what*-WE-*say-He-says* language. Perhaps even the realm of The Sacred might be rescued from dogma and returned to all of us in its broadest expanse – through poetry – if the poets dare to sing wilder hymns.

How else can we begin to free ourselves from the entrenched muck that is currently up to our necks? How can we learn how to live if the words don't live *with* us? (A country that chatters with outrage over *Janet Jackson's breast*, but remains all but silent about repeated displays of Saddam Hussein's killed sons is a country to fear, indeed.) What strange, anesthetic winds have scoured the streets of this nation?

In a free society there is a central place for acute attentiveness, for uncompromising honesty and feeling – and for whatever inspires and sustains them. Enough solitaire. Enough clever ballooning. These are rough days. Desperate times. Times when our language is publicly tortured and forced to mean so much less than it means. There must be a way to stop this dying, a way to make a literature that does more: a poetry with the kiss of a shark and the feet of a sparrow, a poetry at intervals beautiful then ruthless, frank but full of quickening delusions.

– Tim Seibles
February 28, 2004

I

Perhaps only in this fashion do we make visible the submerged magic of the earth and bring closer that culture in which power, knowledge, and achievement recede before the great purpose of life. Which is, as an old Pawnee shaman taught: to approach with song every object we meet.

— Theodore Roszak
The Making of a Counter Culture

Ambition

I. Cow & Microphone

There's so much I can't
make a sound for: sunrise
on a hillside   or a cool dusk
bluing a meadow, late June

or better yet, mid-September,
when the first flecks of autumn
begin to walk summer

down from its tall heat.
How can anything living
not love the color light

spends on October –
when the bulls hum
the last unnibbled pasture?

Wonnnderful! Sometimes I think
I could lend my own true music
to that slow farewell:

the daylight bleeding, a whole season
turning away switching its tail   and my voice,
an encyclopedia of lovely noise,

flies open to the first page, and I'm Ella Fitzgerald's
raging treble clef. I'm a four-legged
fluegelhorn, a glad clarinet, the radical ambassador

scatting a voluptuous river of sax,
blowing the rest of the lows

into a dumb herd, while I run the range
of my whole Angus heart:

   loneliness – the light   always
     a clear view to death   the prevailing
   hands of the powerful   and sweet

    sweet grass – the earth's free bread
  grown back   and lately, the knowledge
    that an animal like me   can't be heard

  exactly – and all this breaks out of my teeth
    into the bovine world. My bruised tongue
  at last an angel's lash

    driving the stampede and   shouldn't I
  be the Pied Piper: my stomachs are full

  of rare news and the cruel promise
    of slaughter. Isn't the other language

  underneath this? Isn't there
    one word   that still brands you?

Further

Childhood is the kingdom where nobody dies . . .
                   – Edna St. Vincent Millay

I used to have feet
bright as a duck's, really.

And a sea-blue shirt covered with ships
that moved. Remember

the sunshine   running the streets
strumming the windows?

Sometimes it was looking for me. Sometimes
it would wait around the maple trees

unlacing the shade while the light
played along the edge,

and I would say *See what I mean?*
But nobody did. And nobody told me

what the clocks were doing.
Other afternoons

it rained. Something that stayed
in my hands. Days

whose names   disappeared.
Gingerbread. Buttermilk.

Musketeers. Words when
words were flavors.

And a silver bicycle
that should have taken me

further   than here.
If I had never

let them   cut my hair
by now   it would be

nearly Oz.

Ago

Awberry Park, June 2002

I don't know where they are now,
Vince and Nahja. Days like these
we'd walk to the park and wrestle
the whole afternoon. Jig-sawed
leaves and yellow grass took over
our free nations of black boy hair.

We were twelve – in the ticklish grip
of just about everything. Nahj loved
red shoelace licorice, and Vince
blacked big **V**'s on the backs of his hands.
Trying to pin those guys was like
trying to braid the tongue of a snake,
and we laughed the way June sun
beams on trombone brass.

I like to believe the craziness
that made us tackle and roll
blew in from a last storm
of childhood genius,
that blind faith in the glory
of playing whatever you want.
But maybe we had just
found a way to rush the time
it would take to shove past
our parents – a way to wait
without waiting for the years
to let us out –
with no homework, no bedtime,
and no reason to clean up our rooms.

This was before we saw
how it was and turned secretly

desperate, before our eyes
were sharpened by sex, before
they killed King   and race
bled all over our lives.
And if Time did anything then,
it only made us younger
or, if it didn't, it only touched us

the way our mothers
brushed our hair, roughly but just
meaning to help us look better.

But it's different now. Nobody
grades my *citizenship*, and my face
won't be smooth again. I can't find
my friends, and when I do, they've strayed
into these half-bald, middle-aged men
whose voices I remember *kind of*,
the way I remember the fried
apples my mom used to fix
when I was still a bacon-headed boy
begging to sizzle along
in the world's hot skillet. But it's
different now,

and it's not the same: these trees
are bigger than the ones we tussled under
and my tough father has grown
smaller than me and kind, and I don't know
anymore. I don't know what I knew
about not getting pinned to the ground,

but one summer when I was half-way
done with my teens, I heard my

great aunt say she didn't like "the flavor
of thyme," and not knowing
any other way to spell that sound,
I stared at the kitchen wall,

at the flowery face of the plastic clock,
and watched the second hand
wheeling its well-worn way around,
and I knew, even then, that somehow,
without really trying, I'd become older
than those hula-hooping little girls
whirling their skinny hips down the alley

and older than I'd been just the minute
before   and I was glad to be made
of that many years, but I did
start to wonder

how it would feel and what
on earth it would mean
when I could actually taste it.

At 41

Houses   House lights

The river's rippled black sheet

Night

Like twinkle from gone stars
memories can be seen long after

Lives missing lives

I would stand beside my mother at the kitchen window

My brother and my father already across the street

One coffee cup with a red-pink lip print
One box of *Kellogg's Country Corn Flakes*

My big brother and my father going to catch the bus

Memory   like a scratch on the brain
over which the needle skips   and skips

How similar the slight sway of their shoulders

The 9th grader   and the biochemist

heading for the S-bus

Was there already something the matter then

What's the matter?

How well they did not talk

"Almost peas in a pod," my mother said
lighting her smile, hand on my hand

October.   Then.

My bones were still growing
but I couldn't feel it –

anymore than I could
understand anything else

I was   actually growing

Visions

after Stephen Dobyns

These are the last days of summer. The sky,
the cool colors of sunset make you think
of things you had wanted to do in July
but put off till August, and now September
leans against your screen door
like the sort of friend you try
to avoid, but who catches your eye, waves,
and comes in.
        A man and his cat step outside.
The cat says *I don't know ablout you, but*
I'm ablout ready to kick someblody in the ass.
This is the way cats confront the weight
of broken promises and perceived injustice.
However, from his position – one hand on the railing,
the ghost-like shadow of an oak branch grabbing
his shoulder – the man sees how flimsy
his life has become. His aching wishes
that dwarfed the city when he was young,
now scrattle and ratch like dead leaves
in a schoolyard.
        The cat says *All these*
sultry sallies out here and don' noblody
wanna help my mojo grow? I got 6"
a' bulgin' hala-lula that say someblody's
glonna get religion and pretty damn soon!
The cat believes in sex and the healing power
of conjoined flesh. He believes the right
kiss could relieve the tongue glitch
that dribbles L's all over his speech.

Across the street
outside the *7-11* the man sees a woman

in cut-off jeans. "Like Mary a little bit,"
he mutters, "her hair curls a little like Mary's."
He remembers certain nights – her apartment,
the almost musical refrain of her hips, the delicious
way they had fit together, pleasure swelling the room
like the smell of good cooking. But it's been years
since he's touched her or even heard her voice, so
what about all those wonderful shapes they'd made?

And for a moment he saw himself from a distance:
standing on the porch, the tree shadow
striping his brown slacks through the railing.
Like a detail you'd catch in a novel, he thinks,
the story of someone beginning
to be older than younger. "I feel
so many feelings," he sighs, blinking
at the furry, block-head of the tom. "Like
a thousand grudges in my heart. Like lemmings
filling the first foot of air off a cliff –
some twisting with regret, some glad, some. . .

        If the cat
could roll his eyes   he would. *Let's go
ovler to the rich neighblorhood and jus'
tear shit up. Let's hurt white people
for no applarent reason.* "Aw,
shut-up," the man spits.

In the man's mind he is flying,
a super-hero suddenly soaring
across orchards and seas. He's the
Green Lantern, and as night inks out day
he watches cities flare up –

the streetlamps, then *Burger Kings*,
bars, marquees, tall buildings downtown.

In his eyes, the kazillion headlights
lace the whole globe in pale gold. It looks
like a thing someone might have
given as a gift, a planet made
for luck – an amulet the size of a world
dangling from Athena's dark wrist.

     You
can kiss my flurry ass, the cat sneers. *I'm*
*glonna get me a Bludweiser. **Then**,*
I'm'a piss on your sneaklers.

But the man wants to know why
living is almost always only slightly
bearable. How had he come to the point
where every day left him swooning
like some chump trapped in a gas station
bathroom? And what did Martin Luther King mean
when he said he'd "seen the Promised Land."

Where had he seen it? Where did it go?

The man tries to picture *the mountain top* –
the huge maples spreading their perfect
purple shade, citizens flaunting only
their fine skins – a place where anybody
could kiss anybody anytime anybody wanted.
But that's not it really, he squints,
there'd be time to disagree. He didn't
want a bunch of naked people
smiling everywhere. He just

didn't want it all to seem
so fuckin' insane.

The man mashes his hand against his forehead
as if microscopic commandos are needling
teeny-weeny bayonets into his brain. He's just
about ready   to make   somebody pay,

    but the cat
bumps his beige head against the man's shin *Hey,*
let's just hang out on the couch.
Let's glo get some tuna flish and
check out some TV. Let's watch Bill Closby
till our skulls collapse.

So that's what they do.
And that's where the man's landlord finds him
days later, staring at the luminous screen
as if into the mouth of God, the mouth
where all the beautiful visions are kept, visions
of what to eat and which computer seems more
personal, which douche is *ph-balanced*, and what trucks
are built *Ford Tough*, the visions showing why
every morning you haul yourself up, and which ice-
brewed beer owns the night, visions of what's
on next   and why you'll like it.

Evidence

Underneath my life

there is another life going on
underneath my life

The sun disappears   It is dawn somewhere else

Everything neatly placed

I finish one thought – I
put it down   like placing

a flat stone   on damp earth

And in the short quiet
another sentence comes

as if I had just picked up a telephone
and caught my voice   trying

a conversation I knew nothing about

The light outside   is the light

that fills the head

of a dead animal   the moment after impact

nearly blue   almost bright

On the one hand there are these things
I just don't understand

On the other   this flat stone
pressed down by people walking past

The kind of stone you lift with the tips of your fingers

and underneath   find a few small openings –
tunnels into the earth –

evidence that something   knew you were coming

Jimi's Blues

after The Band of Gypsys Tour, Spring 1970

Man, I'm just sendin' up smoke signals,
that's all –   'cause it's rainin' *every*where

and it's lonely to be lonely. If I couldn't play guitar
I'd be out there on a megaphone.

When you get down to it
ain' no other music but SOS music,

and if nobody's listening   might as well
get a mirror   and play charades.

When we first hit the scene, they had us
opening for *The Monkees* –

seriously: a million bubble-gummin' teeny-boppers
dying to see Davy Jones,

and here I come, the so-called "Black Elvis,"

black hippie with a white guitar.
You should've seen their faces.

Talk about lonely.

We did this little loose jam
at a street party in Harlem,

and nobody knew me there neither
since *black* radio wasn't playin' the music,

since rock is s'posed to be
a white thing, since the world's gone

skin crazy, but I'm trying
to get some other eyes, you know –

maybe see a color deeper than pain,
bluer than anything you ever knew.

People sayin' "he *gotta* be high
to play like that," but *gotta's*

not a reason. And high
don't take me that far

from here. In half my dreams,
I swear, I'm on this

train – with all these people
tryin'ta sing, but I can't

hear my voice – and somebody says
you're bleeding   then, out the window

I see my mother wave.

That's why playing solos
is like   sendin' up flares. Some nights

I'm not just a message
in a bottle. Nights

when I've actually said something
with my hands.

That's when I hope somebody's
out there   looking for me.

But nobody gets found – and nobody
ever finds paradise, so

people think they gotta die
to get to heaven – which is what

I want the music to be, you know,
a sound that's wide enough

to ride somewhere, someplace
where the weather is better

and you can be with *every*body
all the time – and the words

would be real. Not that
life wouldn't be *mysterious*,

just not as hard to understand,
and maybe I could

put my guitar down maybe
get off-stage for a little while

and think about   just talkin'
like a brand new man.

Meditations from a Small Plane in Bad Weather

Dragonflies.
       Wind chimes.
Chocolate.
       Feel of slate.

If one day your life closed, went
out of business fast –
like the doodad shop near the mall. . .

If it just ended like. a school day –
your life, your life one day   heard, then gone
like a burp – wouldn't you paw at the door?

Cool air –
       wet skin.
Fresh pepper –
       your nose   before a sneeze.

If your heart clammed up
and refused to go on. If dawn roared
but your teeth didn't open – your eyes

unlit, your brain   canceled
like a sitcom – wouldn't you be one
sad, soggy box in Death's damp garage?

That bass thump
       from some punk's *cool car*. Muffin crumbs
stuck to the wrapper. Ants
       bold enough to walk up your arm.

If it came down to the

come-down   and your life came
undone like a blouse, like a zipper –

only this time you could never
get the garment back on – wouldn't you rage

for one red gawk at a cardinal,
for one wool sock, just one more chance

to get your foot inside? Wouldn't you,
for just one more sprained thumb,

wouldn't you, wouldn't you die?

After Awhile

for Haumea

And wasn't the wind   wet like April,
late April – rain blown from the bell
of a blue clarinet.

And Her hair! The dark
guitar of it   and later, the long legs
of sunlight uncrossed,

but unseen. Such instruments!

So many mad edges made into music:

Her arms open   like a storm.
If I didn't want so much
so much, why would I ever

say anything? My heart takes the corner
on two wheels: Her slow walk slow enough

to see by. My mouth harps
and harps, but what

language   is this: dumb notes
in a dumb key. I flame
and I fizzle.

Why am I so sickly and tame?
Even now, Her hips play the world.
Bring my voice! I should praise

like a sax. I should stage
the essential noise –

as if any minute I could die
and the days would forget me.

And won't they?
Isn't it just   a matter of time
till somebody stutters *S-*
S-Seibles   is dead.

I'm already dead.

My life looks for itself in the windows.

And what will I do after awhile?
10,000 years with all these
almost-words still tied in my throat.

Her hair. The strum-drunken tongue of my heart.
Always Her eyes: always
so undarkably dark.

Harvest Moon

Big Sister, apple light, kiss
on the river, tonight
make each word a strange dish,

each long ache, for once, a gotten wish.
Let this small song brush the big dark back
while You stroll along the sky forever.

Yo, to think such bright shadow, this
black sash, that soft shine She wears
comes spun from a sun flung aloft

the other side of my world. What
cat-eyed glow? What well-keyed
mischief? What

slow hands, deft and delicious, undress
my grim predictions, juice up
my ragtime shoes? It happens

on the now, while the moon is unshy.
My soul – yo, otherwise a pale theory – leaps
into the visible, trying his slippery spin

on the glad lap of Earth. Uncles, mothers,
sly lovers, mad friends, the moon does not
come back just to knock our dim efforts,

nor does the river bend away. Wasn't it
this time last year? Remember?
The chubby invitation come soon, soon

each early autumn. Look at the water
with the light jingling like a wind chime
in the shimmer. Turn around.

Our hearts   shine late in the trees.

Fearless

for Moombi

Good to see the green world
undiscouraged, the green fire
bounding back every spring, and beyond
the tyranny of thumbs, the weeds
and other co-conspiring green genes
ganging up, breaking in, despite
small shears and kill-mowers,
ground gougers, seed-eaters.
Here they come, sudden as graffiti

not there and then   *there* –
naked, unhumble, unrequitedly green –
growing as if they would be trees
on any unmanned patch of earth,
any sidewalk cracked, crooning
between ties on lonesome railroad tracks.
And moss, the shyest green citizen
anywhere, tiptoeing the trunk
in the damp shade of an oak.

Clear a quick swatch of dirt
and come back sooner than later
to find the green friends moved in:
their pitched tents, the first bright
leaves hitched to the sun, new roots
tuning the subterranean flavors,
chlorophyll setting a feast of light.

Is it possible   to be so glad?
The shoots rising in spite of every plot
against them. Every chemical stupidity,
every burned field, every better

home & garden finally overrun
by the green will, the green greenness
of green things growing greener.
The mad Earth publishing
Her many million murmuring
unsaids. Look

how the shade pours
from the big branches – the ground,
the good ground, pubic
and sweet. The trees – who
are they? Their stillness, that
long silence, the never
running away.

II

We know we are beautiful. And ugly too. The tom-tom cries and the tom-tom laughs.

> – Langston Hughes
> "The Negro Artist and the Racial Mountain"

Ambition

II. Mosquito in the Mist

You human-types, you
two-legged sapien-sapiens,
you guys are walking smoothies
ta me, milkshakes wearin' trousers,
a cup'a coffee mowin' a lawn.

I gotta hand it to you though –
all the colors, the smells, tall,
petite, skinny-minnies or whoppin'
whale-sized motha'humphries – you
got variety: I'm zippin' around
some summa' nights and it's like
an all-you-can-eat situation.

And I like the threads – hiphop
baggies, halter tops, baseball caps,
culottes – stylin'! And
most'a the fabrics flexible enough
for me and my little straw.

But I sense some chronic
unfriendliness, some ongoing
agitation from you hemoglobes.
My family and me are small things
tryin'a quench a thirst. It's our nature.
The random violence is really
uncalled for. The bashing, the swatting. . .
and the *cursing!* Fuck you guys, man!
It's like you never heard'a the word
compromise.

And the worst

is when you bring down the curtain
right in the middle
of a good suck. I don't think
I need ta spotlight the obvious
analogy, but ok: imagine yourself
alone wit' someone you want
real bad – *her skin is toffee,*
his hair is an avalanche
of dreadlocks – and
the moment
comes: the shared
shimmer in the eyes and you
lean into the kiss, warm
and rich as God's
good cocoa, your mouth's
famished apparatus
slurping up the sweetness,

when – as if from hell's
rabid handbag – a smack,
big as Godzilla, knocks the livin'
juji-fruit outta you.

The luscious touches, the hum
of two hearts, the holy
communion flung
into the fat-ass dark forever.
What? You think we ain't
got feelings!? I got the memories.
It's all in the genes! See,
you big-holes-in-the-face motha'humphries
don't never think nothin'
about other kinds'a life,

but that's ah'ight, I got dreams. I got
big plans. I'm all itchy and bumpy
wit' discontent – and you might not
see it, but I'm gettin' bigger – I
been liftin' – and someday I'm gonna
get a little payback on the go:

land on your cheek like a
roundhouse kick, and before
you can pick up your nostrils
I'm gonna drink you dry, drain ya
to the lees – you'll be
layin' there stiff as beef jerky,
your arrogant balloon
all flat and wrinkly   while I
lift off like a, like a

helicopter, like a goddam
12-cylinda' angel, like a bulldozer
witta' probiskamus big
as a' elephant's dick.

For Handsome George

Things are reversed. . . . One who should be hung. . .
is made emperor. People stand and clap.
— Rumi

When it comes to my country
I'm like a chipmunk   snarling
at an avalanche, like a dragonfly

slamming its sharp beak
into the wilding steel
of an eighteen-wheeler. I hate

to throw my weight around –
bashing trucks, turning back
half a mountain of marauding stone,

but I've got the good reasons. *I* got
the uncounted votes. I have as many
legs as a millipede   which explains

the way I waltz, why some of me
can can-can while the rest of me
just bops. It's hard for me not to

feel perky   with Handsome George
in the White House, with the police

so ready to serenade my profile:
this brown skin, the sexiest rose

in America's garden. And speaking
in-ter-na-tion-al-ly:

why wonder who mighta-coulda?

Let's just globalize. Let's just bomb
everywhere   just in case
some small nation thinks

we ain't got the brass papayas.

I don't like to *exaggerize*. I don't
mean to seem the way I be,

but with this one star-spangled tree
dropping fruit all over, with its
long shade like a collie's lolli-lick

on the glad face of the world,
I wonder how anybody can keep
from crowing *chim chimminy, chim-chimminy*

chim-chim cheree.

The Further Adventures of Tutor the Turtle

Treasent-treasent Treezle-troam
Time for this one to come home.

After all I have told you, Tutah,
are you sure you want to be **black** in America?

> Well, gee, Mr. Wizard, times have changed.
> It might be a little rough, but I'll be down
> with the brothers – they'll show me the ropes.

But, Tutah, look – the Republicans are on the rampage,
white people, in general, seem like dangerous playmates,
and the black community is riddled with   with
self-inflicted wounds!

> Yet and still, Mr. Wizard, I would be African-American.
> I've read about Fannie Lou Hamer and Malcolm.
> Black people are bold and resilient and I wanna *be* one.

> I wanna raise up like Michael Jordan and blow jazz
> with Wynton Marsalis and   and

What, Tutah, what!!?

> And *I wants ta get funked up*, Mr. Wizard – *P-funk:*
> *The BOMB!*

Alright, Tutah, remember *if you hear any noise*
it's just me and the boys:

{the incantation}

Two parts laugh and three parts pain

Cutting lash and hard-won gain

Thumpin' bass and rumble drums
Dr. King and drive-by guns

Skin of dark and spark of eye
Sade's grace and Pippen's glide

Purple Heart and might of back
Time for Tutor   to   be   BLACK!

{Tutor, transformed, disappears into America.
Ten minutes pass.}

HELP, MR. WIZARD!!!

Wha'chu Shoulda // Told the Brother

To be bi-lingual is to be of two minds.
— from a flyer

Yo, nigga, it don't have to be like that – I mean,
a brotha miss a stop sign, he jus miss the mothafucka,
tha's all! It ain't like I hit that raggedy-ass, neva-seen-a-
car-wash, wish-I-had-a-sunroof hooptee on a stick.

If I had I'd halfway understan, but see you can't
give a brotha a break, so fuck you and the two
punk-ass toads you rolled up wit! Lookin like
Dennis Rodman meets Braidzilla – like ta
scared me AND my car: face all scrunched up,
nasty rat teef all snaggly'n'shit –

Gotdam, baby, can't you see it's jus me –
anotha brotha tryin ta keep his eyes on the prize. I mean
I got a lot more than traffic on my mind,
know what I'm sayin? I'm sayin the heat is on, brah,
an' boaf us be deep in the stew. . .

I mean, sometimes, man, all we get
is one chance. Like right now,
at this intersection
with nothing but ourselves
and two cars ready
to take us either way. Maybe

we were supposed to get together:
35th and Colonial, this corner,
like a brief mecca   where stupidity
skids to a stop, where two men

can finally wake up
and recognize each other. Maybe

this was a righteous hiccup
of the universe, brother – the Dharma
in action. I mean, if it wasn't
for this   we'd still be complete
strangers – and I've been

strange enough for long enough
already, know what I mean?

I mean   you see how it is:
how America keeps us
in line, in the line-up,
in the line of fire –
how every sunrise

is another blind corner –
and what it takes *exactly*
to keep these faces.

And what makes us
pretend so hard   to be
so hard. And what

if we do decide to turn
these hands   to blood,
to undo the most sacred thing?

Who's glad? What's fixed?

With everything to lose, brother – what?

Hey Man

. . . this is Talib. You knew me
as Teddy Winborne. When you
get a chance, call me back.

Three calls. Long distance.
Three messages. Like this.

Me and Teddy had grown up together –
listening to Hendrix, playing basketball,
here and there pretending to be *Bruce Lee*.

Teddy had become Talibdeen Bahar,
a Muslim who ran a small insurance office.

We had never called each other long distance.

When we were teenagers
he would say things to his mom
that would have cost me my life.

———————

We used to take the *XH* bus to school.
The Germantown High girls always got on
with their foxy legs in fish-net stockings.

We tried to be cool. I mean, we
weren't scared. We'd say *Hey baby,*

you know   it would be a   Really
dynamite thing   if you and me could maybe
find some time to   lay, play, and parlay.

I guess we were scared, but
we were young brothers in Philly

back in the day of *The Dells* and *The Chi-Lites:*

La-la la-la la-la lalala means
you had to have some lines

like a bridge of silk between you and the girls.

———————

Late '60s, early '70s.
So glad to be black.

Barbers gave us "blow-outs"
to make our 'fros bigger.

Gangs: Dogtown, Haines Street, 12th n'Oxford, The Clang. . . .
When somebody said "Whereyoufrom"
it meant which corner.

Our parents probably should've
kept us in the house
for the rest of our lives.

———————

I'm 40, starting to go bald.
I get back to Virginia and find 3 messages
from Talibdeen Bahar, the once
upon a time *Theodore Winborne,*

who used to play bass loud on his porch,
who had a girlfriend that
nobody ever saw,

who used to shadow his face with a scowl
because you couldn't be "down around the way"
beaming like *Wally and The Beaver* –

you'd have got your ass kicked every day.

And we didn't want that. We wanted to be hard.
We wore high-top *Cons* with silk-and-wool slacks,
copped a Philly stroll, said "Hey, man, fuck that shit."

We thought it would just go on
and on – yockin', boppin' – with us
cooler by the hour.

——————

So, I'm an
inch from calling
him back but the

phone rings my
mother says a
man shot

Teddy yesterday
walked into his

office and some-
thing about $88
killed him
witness said blood

covered his
chair and some

of the floor.

_____

Once, I saw him and Gary jam this mean blues in Melvin's basement.

We were all around 15. Summer. It was hot down there –
like the inside of a fat man's sweat pants.

Cooke flipped into Hendrix, squeezing big howls
from that small guitar. Teddy played bass
with his thumb.

I wonder what Talibdeen Bahar wanted to tell me.

He was bow-legged.
He used to wear baggy khakis.
He was the color of a Hershey's kiss.

Bell Street Blues

Down your mouth   next to the
next to last bend

there's a street named Bell
and a red house

with wooden steps and a skinny
mutt named *Money*

chained to the fence.
And you're in the kitchen

staring into some coffee,
trying to get   how it got

to be like this. Your reflection,
smaller and smaller by the sip.

But 3 blocks west
of your belly, 2 stops south

of your soul. There's a weedy lot
near some cheap apartments –

617 Bell Street: you're upstairs in #3,
eyes caged by the window screen.

A fly keeps   kissing your wrist,
buzzing a loop if you jiggle,

its green shimmer like an itch. When
he looks at you, you see yourself

multiplied many times: each face
smoldering an older shade of blue.

Been sometime since the good times
been around   and the sky is that deep

bruise framed in the windshield with you
trying to drive into the radio:

    The days   be passin   never met one that stayed
    I said the days be sho-nuff creepin   never met one that stayed
    Been runnin roun this ol world   can't seem to find my way

And when you pass some brother who looks
just like you   with his thumb out,

with the sunset blue slung over his bad shoulder
you know   no matter what you do

you're on Bell Street.
Pull over, let him ride:

    I'm so damn tired, darlin   can't hardly tie my shoes
    You know I'm half-way broke-down, baby   can't even tie my shoes
    I mean I'm worn out, sugah   can't even   lace up   dese blues

Lobster For Sale

Over here. in the *aquarium*.
just left. of the fresh fillets.

Save your sympathy.

Usually I'm sleepy. so usually.
I sleep.

And you think. I *dream of the open sea*.

Nope.

When I sleep. I dream.
of sleeping.

Only difference. between this.
and the big drink: in here. it's just. us.

and every hour. I measure. every side.

But sometimes. I see *you*. out there.
eating all that air:

the two-legged mouth.

You think. I'm a. "grocery."

But I don't care. what.

you think.

I keep one thought. one.

I keep it on.   like a night-light.

all day long:

I wish you would. reach in here.
for me.

I wish you. would.

Renegades

Dark until day
day into dusk
like elk
we run

We run like tumbleweeds
like water skeeters

Bright into late
Close until far
we run like
salmon   like radios
like kangaroos
we run

Day into dim
dim until dark
we run

like wolf spiders
like hammerhead sharks

We run like crickets

like moose
like hermit crabs
we run

Dark into dawn
dawnintodusk
we run like like

like tadpoles like
condors like

bacteria
we run

People say, "What?"
We run

People say, "But, but. . . ."
We run

People say,
"Stoprunningoddammit!"

We run like fever
like smoke in a big wind
we run

Our knees pumping high and charged
as the round butts
of hard-bumping lovers
We run

moon into midnight
mist into fog
Carolina into California
We run
like witches like centipedes like
just-about's and maybe's
we run

past McDonald's
past the Chevy Dealer
past the synagogue
we run

Black into white
big into small
bad-ass into buffalo

Read us our rights
We run
like electricity
like frost like jazz clarinet

We run like honey
like blood and milk
We run like
We run like

Chameleons

Do into don't
Dabintosmack
Wouldacouldashoulda
we run

Wolf into woodchuck
Skin into sky

People say, "What?"
We run
People say, "Huh!?"
We run
People say, "Canyou   gettajob
doingthat?"

We run like meals
on wheels like spermatozoa
like shook-up soda

Hit into miss
Road into ditch
Shy into kiss

Like locomotives
like sandpipers
like termites
we run

We run like nobody's watching
We run like nothing's wrong
We run like jackhammers

We run like
We run like

We run like legs on legs
like flying saucers
Hold out your hand
we run

like a kid's nose on a cold night
Bring out the Koran

We run like a tongue up a thigh
naked as sunlight

Like a tattletale to the telephone
we run

You say, "Wait a minute."
We run

You say, *"Stopinthenameofthelaw!"*
We run

You say "Jesus IS Lord!!!"

We run
like a good sweat
like xylophones
like fleas chasing cheetahs
like swordfish
like watercolors
We run like elk
We

Will Not Be Televised

I woke to the timpani of worms tuning the earth.

For the first time ever ever ever
it was Thursday   *really* Thursday.

All my organs were on the outside.

I thumped my intestines – "dookies" inched along
like blind mice brailling a way out.

My liver, the color of a plum.

My kidneys rolled around on their curved backs
grinning suggestively, thighs akimbo – labia
beaming like buttercups.

But it *was* Thursday. I had a job. I
combed. I brushed. I jumped my bike. Bad citizens
harassed me. I pedaled. I pumped.
My ham-flavored lungs flimflamming the wind.

When I got there everyone was retarded:
teachers kept smacking each other with candied yams.

Stop it! Stop it! Stop it!

Students coiled beneath their desks,
flicking out them sandpapery tongues.

I went looking for you with my eyes full of lunch.
I went looking for you unzipped and unafraid.
I roamed the plains with no clear sense of gender.

My organs! My organs, unruly and out in the light,
kept asking, *Is this Freedom? Are we glad?*

I wanted to clench a tulip in my teeth
and wag my head like a wet dog.

I wanted to snap off my arm and bop
some born-again on the prowl.

I wanted John Ashcroft to know how little, how little
we love him.

But by now it was quiet.
And everything that had been left unsaid
sprouted out of the skulls of the unsayers –

beautiful, unscripted conspiracies:

    The friendly aromas of women smiled on the breeze,

        rage blossomed like a runaway broccoli,

    genital laughter filled the broadcasts,

        and the rich   just handed it over.

It was Thursday. *Thursday.*
I stood as close to tears as I was to applause,
and my soul spun aloft like a frisbee.

Ladder

But look! The churches keep opening
their mouths   like trout left to dry in the grass.

And the corporations don't fall down – see
how they run:

the blue suits, the black robes, and their President
whose brain is a bug rolling dung.

Of course, there's blood on the money.

The vampires have always
walked among us.

But so have the trees!

The great stalker called *commerce*
and the Earth's primordial solo
continue to be the windows

through which we arrive – one by one – naked,
splashing like birdless birds into the air,
almost blind, begging to be fed.

Why? To become *this?*
These workaday trolls scared of our newspapers,
revved up ready to buy bigger alarms?

Look how the world rolls around the sun's gold belly,
how the ocean is so much stranger than its word.

Isn't everybody still 3/5ths water?
How lonely   does a truth have to be

before we bring its blues to our lips?

What we do not sing, what we drown in
not saying –

is already music. And still, we keep
turning from the sound

like two-legged animals all buttoned and zipped
unwilling to recognize this tall ladder of bones
to which we cling briefly with our small teeth.

And because we do not see well into the future
because we are busy taking as much as we can get because
money has infected these days with its prolific germ,

what surrounds us looks like forever
but it is not –

just as today's wind
with its grim whistle and bruise
is only the weather for a little while,

on past the dying edge   of the usual
what they said   could never be

begins.

Welcome Home

(An end of the millennium tale)
after Stephen Dobyns

A terrible keening, a collective snarl arose
from the cities and plantations of the world,
and White People, weary of protests and searing
rebuke, simply vanished to the moon.

They were still itchy for conquest, but their burden
had become immense; they felt under
appreciated, even flatly despised. Sociology
dogged their steps. History betrayed them:

A little rape here. . . a little genocide there. . . .

At first, everybody tried to act normal –
Wha'zup, brah? Es todo, ese.
But without the wide awning of whiteness
the sky re-opened like a Nigerian bazaar

and people began to dawdle before mirrors,
to lolly-gag around store windows: Inexplicably,
their complexions seemed lighter.

The global blizzard under which whole
villages had been buried, whole civilizations
lost   was finally over, and marigolds
blazed all over the dark citizen rainbow.

The huge white hand that had been day and night
squeezing their heads was gone and everybody
turned off their TVs. Why watch police shows?
Why dilly-dally around with self-hatred and

dumb distraction. Gang members plunked down

their automatics and started glee clubs. Ministers
admitted they knew nothing about God and
began to breast-feed in public to prove
they were starting over. Everywhere bars
closed down. Drug dealers slashed
prices, but finally had to think in terms of tofu,

for without whites and the triple psychosis
of "color gives privilege gives power"
everyone started untying their shoes.
No more *Tums*, no more *Tylenol*.
No more mashing two faces into one.

Those who had spent their lives *trying
to be white*   whapped each other
with blobs of pizza dough and started
12-step recoveries. Each meeting
started with a chorus of *I like this ol'
skin a'mine   and I'm gonna let it shine*.

After nine months the Black Separatists reacted:
They held rallies, displayed white mannequins
in hostile poses, passed out **Remember
Rodney King** billy clubs. They took over government,
sharing control with the Latin-Asian Assembly.

A new draft was begun to induct those
who would pretend to be members of the
KuKluxKlan – unlucky people forced
to wear pointy hoods and shout *"Amurrika
fer Amurrikans"* and *"Ah sher as hayul
hate me some melon-eatin porch monkeys!"*

58

Eventually the Nation of Islam seized power
and, with AIM soldiers as allies, ran around
sloshing non-believers with white paint.
"You're one filthy caucasoid," they'd sneer
tugging their bow ties.

"Quit messin' up our duds," people
smiled. "The world is a symphony. Our lives
are the music. We shan't again be what we were."

For, without White Supremacy and its
soul-eating whispers, the old rage
that had simmered everywhere
like crocodile soup
was covered with foil and stuffed in the fridge.

The *shop-till-you-drop* frenzy
intended to distract people
from the cruel parade quickly sputtered.
Why fill your apartment with anything
but gladness? Why chew on the past?

A rash
of poly-cultural lovefests
swept the globe: Ugandans orgifying
with Filipinos while the Apache covered
their Eskimo cousins with butterfly kisses.

In the third *Year of Ease*,
with the help of Colon Powell
and a few other republicans of color

a coalition of corporate types seeped into office.
Donning Armani suits they shuttled to the moon
where The Whites were sitting around, listless,
blending into the pale landscape.

With time on their hands like a stain –
and no egg foo young and no one to teach them
how to rap – the majority grew somber: "Perhaps
we went too far," they nodded. "That stuff
with the Indians. . . . Those bombs on Japan. . . . We did
get a little crazy with the   *slavery* thing."
Their children scowled, "What on earth
were you thinking!? It's no fun on the moon!"

The **R**ainbow **B**usiness **C**oalition
asked around until the leader, Bob Robertson –
an international televangelist – waved his hand.
He'd made his fortune dealing Krugerrands
and sat fondling a crucifix.

"We just happened to be in the area,"
the RBC said. . . figured you might
need   a change of scenery   maybe some tacos?"
Bob breathed hotly, buffed the cross on his vest.
They felt awkward. Juan Valdez hummed
a little blues. "It'd sure be nice," Colon shuffled,
"to have hockey again."

Over the moon's west edge their planet,
crowned in sunlight, crested like a whale.

"Affirmative action – *assmirmative* action,"
Justice Tommy added, "After all, what else
are bootstraps for!?"

"Ha-lay-loodoo," Bob sang, "let me pow-wow
with the others."
                    Back on Earth the RBC
argued and begged, invoked Buddha and Jesus,
infiltrated the Baha'is, sent their faithful
door-to-door. "Imagine being white," they sighed,
"and nobody wants you around –
just because of that. Ha-lay-loodoo! Friend,
prejudice is pus in the heart!"

After a year's debate a kind of probation
was set up. Jobs would be created or
"workfare" required for those
of lunar descent. No more teams
named *Indians*, etc. No more
Pat Boone covering *Little
Richard*, etc. A snowy day
in July would be set aside for the
celebration of White History.

This is how they returned:

First, the weather was adjusted, cooled.
Madonna, Elvis, Frank Sinatra and The Stones
were smuggled back into music stores.
VO-5 and *Cosmopolitan* glimmered
on the racks. Billboards offering one
well-dressed, red-haired, smiling
Caucasian sprang up. Then
the public service announcements:

    "When you see someone *white*

do not be alarmed   This is only a ***test***.
Think ***diversity***."

The preparations went on and on
until, after the seventh solstice, people
began to suspect that the whole thing
had been a hoax, that maybe *whiteness*
itself was a myth. It was hard to
recall   what it was like with them
in the world. Maybe it hadn't
been so bad. Maybe they were too
terrible to be clearly remembered.

Then, came a shining in the air, a soft
switch in the wind, a stillness as though
before a sneeze. And Whites began
to fall from the sky – in a spotty drizzle
at first – a girl scout, two
skiers – then a steady shower and soon
it was pouring White People. Whole
suburbs and villages, whole nations – the heavens,
like a celestial Europe, opened up.

And, as the new light flickered
on the Dutch, the Spaniards, the
brown-haired Slavs, the bright-eyed
Brits, and finally, on the complicated faces
of those who'd become *American*,

the inhabitants of Earth
cried out, lifting their arms
to catch the strange, familiar bodies.

III

The technocracy is not simply a power structure wielding vast material influence; it is the expression of a grand cultural imperative. . . a capacious sponge able to soak up prodigious quantities of discontent and agitation, often well before they look like anything but amusing eccentricities or uncalled for aberrations. . . .

Yet what else but a brave (and hopefully humane) perversity can pose a radical challenge to the technocracy?

— Theodore Roszak
The Making of a Counter Culture

Ambition

III. Primate, Bipedal

This: to find no distance
between what I am and what I seem.
To catch myself between myself

and the mirror   unafraid,
afraid of everything, *everything*.
To not have History
scaling my face.

To break the thumbs
that hung the world. To tear those hands
with these dull teeth. Human

almost. To hate. To reason. To burn,
while the Sphinx feathers my ear

saying, saying *who   are you   talking to?*

This: to be pure
animal – my blood
unlocked, my legs

scribbled with hair, my soul
perched on my shoulder. Free.
Unconvinced   of my name: on my tongue,

for the first time, salt.

To chase this   then *be* this,
then sleep. This. I want *this*
to be my life: to come back

with a mouth ready
to send new noise.
To learn again

how to stand, how to put one foot
down   then the other a little farther along.

Land Ho!

for the New World

Like this when.
When it could have been
   otherwise.

When *otherwise*
might have risen to the surface
like a fish   like a bubble
on the blue lips   of a blowfish.

Like a complete city
   floating by in a bubble –

bright black streets, big-
brimmed hats, sleek denim slacks,
millions of shoes and sashes –

   boating by in a bubble
strapped to the back   of a junebug
on an otherwise
   normal day.

   Ahhrrg! Avast ye, maties:

A day! Just grab you one!

A sky full of sky and otherwise,
wilder still – air, as much
as you want, more than you
could ever breathe. *Yohoho!*
One ubiquitous lunch it be.

And squeezing thru the seams,
unrecorded, unconsidered things –

spiced and languorous, but
so alreadily delicious:

like a sweaty runner –
between her legs, an afternoon
sweet as an ocean swizzling

under summer's orange kiss:
the slow aromas wafting ashore,
so bold, so unforgivably welcome.

   Ahoy! Ahoy!

And you are there
with we are there
    with sandpipers!
    And their piccolo beaks!

And two tubas   threatening
to play the beach, the tubists themselves
all a-tango, circling lockstep left
and true, sunshine shocking the blue brass.

So close. So ready. So
nearly music. The melody
like the sultry tip of a tongue
just one candlewick
    from your ear. *Ahoy!*

Such almost voices, so agonizingly
otherwise. So utterly and deep.
Like this. We could have lived
    like this.

Not Spoken

As if thirst were not a wound.
As if the thirst for company were not a wound.

Consciousness   the one shadow
from which light grows.

As if all the ache flowed from the same bruise.

Near dawn. My blood caught in its circle
I think of your body   your legs opening

And the light hairs strung along your wrists.

As if your shoulders.
As if the muscular turn of your hips.
As if I could tilt your mouth
to this dent in my chest.

So, bit by bit, it becomes unmistakable.
This not knowing   how to say.

As if I had already broken
into the last room   and found the words
still not English.

As if being flesh were not call enough.

Why stay here to be American?

Where what is exactly sexual   has no country.

Let's go.
Whole words. Whole worlds slow

between us. Trying to pronounce themselves.
Unlost.

The body, the one sacred book.

My hand. My hands know
so little of your hands.

The names of pleasure   held

in chains   taken in ships.

Refugee

Landed.   Here.

My brown skin   like a noise.

Between two mouths

a Temple: one kiss

and I have no name. I give it

away. I step

out of an hour: wait for The House

in my blood

to open

Bonobo

Bonobo apes employ sex – all kinds – as their primary
mode of social interaction. Violence is virtually
unheard of among them.

Call Drea and Carlo   Jareeta, Josefina and George.
Ring Zhao, then Yusef   Dvora, Savannah and Dee.

Let's not be so useless today. Let's find a field
and, Andre, bring some birds – a thousand sparrows

to pepper the sky, a ruckus of toucans for color.
And Renée, don't forget the sunlight and no more

than 75 degrees with the friendly breeze that sings to us.
José, we stand in a place where no one can run naked,

but the police go public with their billy clubs and guns.
Red automobiles might be waxed and shown off,

but the genitals are locked up, gaberdined, touched
in secret and dubbed "privates." Let's not mingle

with the *forgive-me-my-sinners* or their grim
and constipated God. Jeanette, make sure the field

is a quilt of monkey-grass and periwinkle.
Send the numbskulls to the city for a shopping day.

Then, let's get with the kisses –
who with who, who cares? Who cares!

As long as the lips are excellent
pastries and the tongues, circumspect

and merciless. It should take half a day
to spill the vulva's quick honey   longer

to key the restless clarinet of the cock – half a day
or the sun will consider the good light wasted on us.

And why not be deliberately lazy with the buttery rays
like a broth ladled over us? Why not a languid

and mellifluous career grooving hallelujah with our hips,
as if this flammable symmetry were a ship always

turning between the two ports: *wanting* and *having*.
Don't let Masala and Sissy double-up

on Susanna. Watch out for JT and Bernard.
Tell them to hold their horny horses –

tell them   *the orgasm, like a favorite*
auntie   always saves a place at her table,

the dinner ready whenever we arrive.
But nobody can stop them. Who can ever stop

any of us   and why: as if we haven't already lost
too much time working –and too many lives.

So let there be lots of licking, every mouth
on loan to the loud song of our loneliness,

and fucking, of course – crisp, proud, posh,
preemptive, unimpeachable, forever and ever –

from these front yards to Zimbabwe and the Taj Mahal,
fucking in the loosest, most elaborate sense

of the word. Forget the word. Let thighs be questions
and other thighs be answers. When we're true like this

even the sky rolls onto its back, even the most reluctant
shade slides over us: Eros in the air – bold fish

stroll from the lake, a lone bonobo brings a symphony
of oboes   spilling all the unsaid things.

Let's take this one chance and be terribly
kind to each other. I'm sick of wafting around

like a fart in the attic. Leave the money
to the morticians and their cadavers.

Let's make the most noise with our hearts.

In a Glance

I'm caught in this curling energy! Your hair!
Whoever's calm and sensible is insane!
— Rumi

The unseeable   seen! – that saxophone
spilling from the window – a true *very soon*

held between two lips: Her smile   for no reason
a carnival quietly placed   a flaze
made to bathe in   the right door gliding
belightedly up the boulevard:

All day my heart face-down my pulse
pecking like a chickadee sick of its
short wings I had hoped some astonishing

would scratch the gravel from my eyes:
sunset hatched from a soup can   a tree toad
tap-dancing with a tadpole. . . . Perhaps
a meat flag   fricasseed above

my dumb country   but never the burning wheel
of a slow hour: Her smile   a glass blown *yes*
two maybes dressed in a wish –   three buttercups

in a jade vase under a blue umbrella

a cello ablaze with me drawing myself
along the strings Her smile plays:

To feel so much!   But not go mad enough
to shuck the grave in my skull   to scrub
and bumble for the glum Puppeteer

while my heart my teeth my
orthopedic verbs strain
like mice in a scrum

My voice! bruised and shoeless
goes mumbling the streets
trying to buy a vowel

My alphabet used to be 10 feet long –
every letter a xylophone a shark's leg a
flubber ballooning my whole soul a holler
from the blind church of the unsaid: *Her smile,*

sly melody glad enough to fling the grass afire
kind season that rings the light beyond Her lips:

But soft! Me, a man collided, the both the between –

the lovely shape of a mind unshaved by reason –
over the over   banging into the change

Late Shift

Places –
maybe dreams

from which I cannot   return: the velvet

touch of Her lips, first light
fingering a cup: sacred dislocations

of mind – the way the right sound
becomes visible.

Where I am now
it's later – the clocks have been amended

to include all the strange hours –

and Someone cracked my name
as if all my life I'd been locked inside.

I know the shelves stay stocked, big cars lead the chase,
there's always more   and more to eat.

But was that ever   *my* country?

I was.   born there.
And I'd go back   if I could –

just to feel less lonely –
but what I took

to be a certain distance

was actually a late   shift in myself,

a different kind of listening:
the voice, a thread of honey –

the jar tipped   just enough to one side:

Listen.

We belong to no nation.

One day we will hold the earth
again   as if She were a love

nearly lost, Her rainy hair tangled in our hands.

The soul is what we are.
Every life   a word the wind turns to say.

And though trouble grows back like a beard,
an unchained blood governs my tongue.

I have seen the door   that is not there

still open

Anthem

for Aditi

I would have a new name –
all vowels and two m's –
to which I would come
when You called. No, no word

but a stitch of wind,
a light come-hither
in the billowing trees, the fizz
of fresh ginger-ale: that

would be my name.
A trellis of nothing
but shadow, a cup
of smoke, the glare
of something broken,

call me *that*,
and I will arrive
like a season the size
of a hand, like the smell
of hot soup, I will be
where You are –

my shoes empty,
my voice knocked
sideways, my tongue
buttoned all wrong
like a little boy's shirt.

Woman, I'll never find my name,

nor an anthem for this
starved country in my chest,

but if that *might*   bring me
the taste of Your mouth
I will keep trying to sing

because this near music, this
time spent drowning, this one

small shining amidst all the worry
is still paradise. I swear

on the blood of my soul
I've seen the proof: a good world

spoken twice in Your dark eyes

and the perfect democracy
of sky   spilling over

the citizens and the shape
of Your lips   and Your smile

which must be my lost name.

First Kiss

for Lips

Her mouth
fell into my mouth
like a summer snow, like a
5th season, like a fresh Eden,

like Eden when Eve made God
whimper with the liquid
tilt of her hips –

her kiss   hurt like that –
I mean, it was as if she'd mixed
the sweat of an angel
with the taste of a tangerine,
I swear. My mouth

had been a helmet forever
greased with secrets, my mouth
a dead-end street a little bit
lit by teeth – my heart, a clam
slammed shut at the bottom of a dark,

but her mouth pulled up
like a baby-blue Cadillac
packed with canaries driven
by a toucan – I swear

those lips said bright
wings when we kissed, wild
and precise – as if she were
teaching a seahorse to speak –
her mouth   so careful, chumming
the first vowel from my throat

until my brain was a piano
banged loud, hammered like that –
it was like, I swear   her tongue
was Saturn's 7th moon –
hot like that, hot
and cold and circling,

circling, turning me
into a glad planet –
sun on one side, night pouring
her slow hand over the other: one fire

flying the kite of another.
Her kiss, I swear – if the Great
Mother   rushed open the moon
like a gift and you were there
to feel your shadow finally
unhooked from your wrist.

That'd be it, but even sweeter –
like a riot of peg legged priests
on pogo-sticks, up and up,
this way and *this*, not
falling but on and on
like that, badly behaved
but holy – I swear! That

kiss, both lips utterly committed
to the world   like a Peace Corps,
like a free store, forever and always
a new city – no locks, no walls, just
doors – like that, I swear,
like that.

Orgasm

It is the place
not seen

The secret
kept and unkept

The place we want
too much

The far place   near

That song you make

that reckless
pitch, the muted

cry that tells
how long you've

wandered and how

far: when
did you learn? How

do you know
what to say

each time you arrive

finding the river
deeper and the unvisible
bridge across

Someone Else

She had on a long dress, twilight blue
and buttoned down the back, black buttons
sewn with yellow thread   and new sandals,
and the air dozed, warm, early May, early evening –
the day about an hour from dusk.

And she had a long stride; you could tell
she worked somewhere that made her
move quickly, but now she had showered
and come outside   eating a cookie – oatmeal

raisin – and as she slipped one curved edge
between her teeth, you were nervous
about what you might say. You believed
that words could be important, that

certain sentences could change
the space between you and this
one woman   until something
had to touch. It's funny:

just before Easter she had shared a table
with a man who probably taught algebra.
The café was crowded. Twice their knees
had brushed. The page he leaned over

held difficult equations. She started
skimming her ankle along his shin
until she found herself wet. There was
something about the dare in doing it

without permission, without his ever
looking up and, to be honest, you also knew

that speaking was usually a cool fidget,
a fig leaf: you simply wanted to kiss her,

her legs which you had seen last Saturday
in shorts. Without a word, you wished
you could press your lips to her legs
to feel the muscles flex and settle –
if only once – against your mouth.

And you thought, for a second, she might
be wearing nothing but her something-
like-cinnamon smell underneath that dress,

which takes you back   to the once
upon a time   when you were young enough
not to know what to do with what you wanted:

one night late   the laundry room   quiet
except for the spinning dryer. Lucinda

sat on a *Maytag*, unknotted the drawstring
of her baggy plaid pajamas, and dared you –
put your mouth   right here – so you did it,

kissed open the caramel flower with your
scared lips   while room by room above you
the dormitory studied and slept.

In fact, this woman, *Ms. Long Stride*,
had also been thinking about sex,
about the way her first lover didn't take

her underwear off, but tugged them
to one side with two fingers, untying
the hour with his kind hands.

And that sudden sleep afterwards,
when she would close her eyes to the surge
and fade of five o'clock traffic: the connection
between her and the ever-raging scramble

broken   under the sumptuous weight
of good company. And at times
you have believed the sexual world

was made for this, for traveling
to exactly what you mean, across
the long separateness, the racked
stammers   into the body's only passages.

So, you thought you should
say something   if there was a chance
to become more than a stranger –
though your strangeness, like everyone's,

is all you really have. There are
the loving illusions of being familiar,
of entering *a relationship*, and words
do make the boundaries

less definite, make it almost possible
to understand someone else, to see
someone composing himself
between inflections and breath

meaning to say   how it is
what it is   and why this
wanting equals
what it does.

Instead, you asked her the time
and stumbled some dumb song about
warm weather and summer coming.

And she was thinking things too, showing
the watch on her wrist   and the careful
reach of her voice: her own odd history
telling her   what not to say.

Once, at a birthday party where you became
39   a good friend sat on the sofa
slyly revealing the flimsy underwear she wore.

One knee would drift away from the other,
and she'd laugh – the soft gloss of purple silk
barely lit by the lamp in the corner.

And later you lay in her bed watching her
take off your pants in the wall-sized mirror,
watching how, with her lips wet, she

leaned over the slight curve of your cock
and you saw your face for a second
given back by the glass,

so you *were*   someone else, being there,
her legs around you, her body

repeating its luminous phrase, as if
to clarify everything. And you understood then,

that this was what would blaze inside your skull
years after your life was over: that taste,
her mouth, the nearly spoken –

the moments when your body became
an invitation, a window, a way   to admit
the weary angels: other people, sweet companions –
the one inscrutable word   rushing into your arms.

Spoken

for Renée

It could already be years ago.
Yesterday evening, the beach,
the jeweled goddess of water

curling   uncurling for miles her hair,
while towards the east edge of earth
two thunderheads unfurled the pelican moon.

Seeing you there, a woman made of ocean
and the darkish air naming dusk,
I could not say how glad I was

for your life in this life, this America
adrift her sharky machines –

with all her citizens so carefully
netted, then told they are free.

And the great liquid forest,
the unfinished argument of tides – remember

the insects   sizzling the dune grass,
the new words the gulls kept trying to say –

how can there be speech   for anything?

Your sleek beauty.
Plovers zigging the ragged cuff of foam.
Your hands. Loneliness

and the loneliness to come.
Your skin, like a voyage. One kiss,

like a change in the wind. The human alphabet
hoisted to catch   one true glimpse of the true.

How impossible it is   to praise exactly
the revelation of someone you love,

how strange to remain among the living,

and how lucky to speak – no matter
how well – luck's nameless holy name.

IV

The world has grown huge and cold. Surely this is the moment to ask questions, to theorize, to speculate, to wonder out of what materials a human world can be built.

– Richard Wright
"Blueprint for Negro Writing"

Ambition

IV. Virus: Confessional

Not every i-
dea
that thrives
is a good
idea and just
because
you build a house
and say
here
lives *The True*
doesn't mean
it ever
moved in: e-
ven if you
make books
that tell ama-
zing stories
about how
it's neces-
sarily so:

Bad things
almost never an-
nounce themselves
as bad, no
matter how much
you wish
they would.
In fact,
evil is just
good recon-
sidered: Sometimes

what seems
brutal
really just
wants to
get a-
long and regrets
what must be
done in
the name of
its chur-
ches and schools:

Take me, for
example. You prob-
ably think I'm
heartless,
but when I
come to your bo-
dy I don't
want trouble. I'm
just making con-
verts, I just
want to be
where everyone
believes,
where we
can share and
share a-
like. No one
likes be-
ing alone. I
work for U-
topia. I dream

of America,
how it began
with a few
strang-
ers who
wandered into
a beau-
tiful place and
decided to
make it
freer and
brave and now
look at the
cities: neigh-
borhoods, neon ma-

chinery, straight
streets, people who
need peo-
ple, all
that sun-loving
glass.

Nausea

Some people will
go accidentally, others

will go hungry, but a lot of us are going
to be killed *on purpose*.

Who can disagree? There's an old
new dance

all over. Even the knives

understand. The victims, their numbers
lined into phone books: who'll get

all the free time
they were going to spend?

Maybe it will be my hurry that
murder interrupts   or an old photo

of you blurred in the obituaries   a cousin's

handsome curves outlined in chalk,

while a few not-quite witnesses turn
serious for the well-dressed mike.

And always the grown-up
resolve, the *hanging*

in there, that obedient
rush   into another day.

The human world says *come on*, says *get ready*

for work it says   and we trot into the teeth –

our soft flesh available completely, blood
swerving in our veins.

And it happens, happens always   and sometimes
with the sunshine describing the wounds

exactly.

Our somewhat skinny luck
fending it off

for awhile, but the calendar has plans, plans
ahead

for every one   or ten of us
and who doesn't go

where the calendar says? Even when the killing hums
right next to your ear.

It'll turn into news   and the news
moves around.

Look around.
The weekdays still wait in their rows.
And almost

no one is screaming. Why not
call some friends? If you can

call your mother.

Listen   to the calm hello.

Matrix

The Matrix is the world pulled over your eyes.
— Morpheus

Chain link. Chain saw.
Traffic jam. Work.

Single? You can hear the engines
smacking their lips.

Nice car. Big mall. Really
nice. Attaboy! Love is

a heart attack. Have you

seen me? I've been on
my day off. Cool. Yo, baby,

yo: you and me
could be fast food. Do any fries

come with that? Thank God
it's Friday! "Obey

your thirst!" It's so
easy to do. An extra-large

cross on every corner. B-b-b-
bite me. When do you get

off? Still single? Call *1-800-*

THE-LOST. Have you
seen me   having a

great career? Must be

somebody out there
I can love. I'd like a wife —

double-meat, no cheese. Jesus!
I could eat that all day. You better

get to work. Is that

the *chicken?* We're getting
married! We'll have extra love

all the time. Yo, baby, yo: we're
sooo excited for you! When's the Happy

Meal? Have you seen me —
having a baby and some

fries? That'll keep you busy.
Nothing like having a

burger of your own. B-b-b-bite
me. Work + children = free time.

Have a blessed day. I guess
I better

get that *to go.* Who's next?
An extra day off

in every bite. Have you

been saved? Can that be all
you can be? Be all

that you can be. Join the

hamburglers. Cool! Finally
got a minimum job with a

medium drink. Do you ever get

the feeling? Sometimes it's
hard to say. Are you

m-m-m-married? Are you

l-l-l-lonely? Have you
been putting on

a few quarter-
pounders? B-b-b-bite me. Make me

proud of myself while earning extra
pickles for college. Horny? Yo,

baby, yo: let's get married. Let's obey
the thirst. Let's get to work and

supersize! Let's have
so many children that we live

in a shoe. Let's McBelieve
the McBiscuits grow

on trees. An all beef

patty in every pulpit.
Cool. Love   is getting some

time off. Is that the

original chicken? Who
put you

on the cross? I'm off
every 3rd Tuesday. I keep

trying to get off,
but mostly I get extra

crispy. What's for
dinner? Have you

seen me? Lately?

Christmas 2001

Work and Win! (bumper sticker)

Someone ties two blue balloons to your eyelids:

Rise and shine! The new sun
smears the dark like a paw: Tuesday –

just like last week, Tuesday   and hurray!

It's still America still   with all the flags
with 'tis the season   and that   that thing

in the White House: *Ho-ho-ho.* Death,

like oil   gushing, like a mouthful
of mistletoe, like honey

on your fingers, like a population not

actually thinking: You're beginning to understand this

is what happened   to freedom: dumbfuckery

in the first degree   and big cigars
in all the offices: *On Dasher! On Blitzen!*

Bizzy: Santa's little soldiers. *Semper Fi:*
Your bashful taxes dressed up and deployed

whenever, wherever your country gets interested

in protecting your interests, the ones you
wished for: one vote / one wish:

one wish per citizen – every vote a kiss
on the plump cheek of a nation

that sang   like a dim- ah- kris- ee
but often acted like something

unrelated: If a dumdum round

ripped open your head

right now   they'd find one of Snow White's dwarves –
Dopey or *Sleepy* – still spinning the wheel

as if this had been a fairytale all along: Once

upon a time   you *fa-la-la-la-la*

felt lucky to be American – and, of course, you
of course, you are:

Clean water, animals glad
to be meat, Michael
Jordan, MTV, *Harry Potter*
books to read, and jobs: *your*

job – a jobby job, a job to live for:

Get up up up!

But this morning   there's a kind of light
that fits like a door   closing on the world

like getting older, like a cold you

can't quite cure, like the Official Smile and news
from Jerusalem, like a suicide bomber

in Chicago   fingering directions, dashing through the snow

Playing Catch

for Hermann Michaeli

On the day the balls disappeared,
men playing soccer suddenly looked

like lunatics chasing the invisible
rabbit. Pro baseball players became more

clearly what they'd always been: bored
teenagers waiting for some action.

Spectators, at home and in the stands, believed
they were being jerked around by a player

conspiracy, that this was the first whiff
of another strike that would cancel all the fun.

On the day the balls disappeared, the sun
did not sneer above the dust-drenched rooftops

as if *this* were a day to keep your finger on.
And if all the refs overslept that morning,

it only meant they were a little extra tired
of instant-replay highlighting their best mistakes.

In fact, it was a Saturday, sunlight
the color of a canary. Nearly *every*body

was outside! I remember one woman especially –
alone in the schoolyard taking jumpshots:

her mouth shaped an O

every time she left the ground.

It had been August for more than a month
and the televisions were jam-packed:

pre-season football, rugby, golf, even softball. . . .
If you didn't know better   changing

channels   could make you think the world
was a giant field   divided by white lines and water,

that life was mainly a chance to fall in love
with one of the many man-made spheres.

I guess they went all at once
or at least within the same 15 minutes.

I'd been watching the U.S. Open
when Pete Sampras, ready to serve,

gestured to a ball-boy who quickly
pointed to another, hoping not to be

blamed. Some Swedes in the cheap seats
began to whistle. I went

to the fridge and grabbed a plum.

But I remember   outside my window
a boy and his sister playing

catch: he waved a new red glove. She
was a lefty and brown as coffee and,

just to show off, she whipped the pitch
a foot above his reach.

A moment later he yelled, *I can't
find it – I don't see it – it ain't*

out here! She figured he just
wanted *her* to go get it. She thought

he was just messin' around.

Invasion of the Body Snatchers

A lot of building and violence. The wars.
You tortured each other.

You thought you understood
what money meant, what money
wanted, but you never imagined.

The things done for the sake of country.
For the sake of *race*.
Labor.
The carefully broken wheel of class.

You all had been so energetic and determined –
so plump with what we named "Freedom"

The jobs were everywhere.

When the televisions first came on
you were ready to sit down and watch.
You must have been almost praying

for someone to save you, to send
the worries away. We gave you
religion. There wasn't any big
hurry, but by the time

there were 3 stations and color
it seemed like you really wanted it

our way   to see and believe, to
laugh, laugh, laugh, to become

a faithful shopper –
another day   another dollar:

That's a pretty simple prayer.

And gosh, look how bright it stays out there!
All the friends want *cable* now.
Shouldn't everyday be as Saturday as this –

the sun so blonde it's making everybody blind.

Do you ever catch yourself wondering
what they're thinking – *other people*,
how they keep coming to work so calm?

Some   you used to know. Some
were just like you. Remember:

those soaring conversations? Your hands
open to the speed of words,

as though you could actually
hold them: your ideals –

the will to do *Good*, to claw
evil's clean-cut company face, the
we shall overcome   and all that.

Well, you needed to be born again   so you were.

Sometime between civil rights and *Oprah*,

somewhere between Vietnam and *Desert Storm*.

Remember how Baghdad lit up that first time –
all the "sorties," and here, the yellow ribbons –

weren't you almost feeling   kind of glad?

You think all this has something to do with *Republicans?*

Look at your watch,
how those thin hands move you around:

it's like you're floating, like you're

not really here now.

You think there's something strange in the water?
You think there's some new germ in the air?

Think fewer trees   just mean   fewer birds?

I guess we'll see.

Dem Dat

for Subcommandante Marcos and the Zapatistas

Before them that's got will take their lovely feet
off da necks of dem dat don't, before a good vine
can uncurl one itsy-bitsy leaf, *sweet blood gonna
turn black in da street.* It's an old story but even
when it was a youngster, *wif teeny little legs,*
nobody was listening. *Dey wanted dem pretty
stones. Them wanted to yum-yum da money.*

Maybe somebody started the wrong church.
Could be one late afterdark fierce mice
bum-rushed their hearts: mouse junta?
Or could be dat mashed cricket thing, you know:
one of 'em get in ya shoe, ya put it on –
cricket gets all masherooed, but that weren't
no bug; dat was yuh soul.

And the soldiers who grin, los brave ones who fire
on peoples who got nuttin' but sticks – somebody
buys their uniforms. Somebody yanks their strings,
and rubs their tummies: *Somebody wif sacks'a*
NAFTA bucks in they back pockets.

Some blood will paint the walls of shacks. *Some
friends already be sittin' in El Presidente's lap.*
He feeds them American cheese; *they feeds him*
da brown eyes of chil'ren, the crushed thumbs
of cheap labor. I don't know. *Maybe da rich
been raised funny,* but that's an old story too –
just ask the Sandinistas. *Yeah, acks Guatemala.*
Ask The Shining Path. *Shit, acks anywhere!*

It walks on big legs now, big hairy legs
wif big yella corns on da feets. And still,

nobody wants to hear it. *'Specially not*
wif stars n' stripes n' burgers n' fries
all scrumptiddlyumptious ev'ywhere: how
can a good citizen cogitize proper-like
wif Chickum McNuggets all twixt
his and her teefs?

Who run Fort Knox?
Who makes dumb money
when the bombs get smart?
Economics is all boil and bubble
scramblized wif strangeness.

I worry what Zapata would say
about this, about the funny,
funny way   the news keeps
blaming the hands of *dem dat*
don't got. I guess my country's
all cuddled up with that stuffed
monkey from Texas, *but maybe y'all*
need a jestah, so don' nobody see
*who doin da **big** pimpin', who*
dealin da dirty dirt.

But the truth   *is da troof,*
and some skinny spirit *gonna sing*
a fat-ass song pretty soon. Somebody's
got to fit these good birds back into the wind.
Yeah, someday dat someday gotsta come
one day, don't it?

116

Back

for R.E.O.

This always happens:
sometime
after the day you
are born   somebody
does something
to you.

And it's bad
and hard
to believe, maybe
leaves a mark. Not a
visible thing
necessarily, but

something
like a scratch
inside one lung
that
burns a little
when you breathe.

A lot of times it's
been some time
since
it was,   since
the thing
was
what it
was,
since the thing
was done   and over
the years you've

said *I'm*
okay. I'm al-
right. Could'a
been worse.

And yeah, it
could've been. Yeah.
But you *are*
fine now. You are. You
go days, weeks,
longer   with hardly
a trace. You
work, make
love, joke
around.

Like always, people
ask how you've
been   and you
flick it off
your bottom lip:
fine. It's so auto-
matic – as if, of
course, the
past
with its jagged
bulk could sleep
inside that
small word.

But when you
do   think about it,
your eyes trace

a certain
curve in the air
and your stomach
is full of
stomach and

whatever *it*
was   finds you and you
cannot stave off
the fact
that the human
world *is*
an unbearable place,
that really nothing

is okay,
none of it, no
bones ever
knit.

And though it's
good to seem
friendly – nice
to let the
bygones go – right
then,
what you need
more   is to find the
one, the ones

who did *what*
it was and do it
back
to them, give it
back.

Night Flight

After awhile everything is a metaphor for everything.
　　　　　　　　　　　　　　 – Mark Cox, from a conversation

By the feel of things, this dark
must be rough. The jet strides
and scuffs the air the way someone
might walk a crowded row
in a movie theater – here
and there bumping a knee,
stubbing a toe – and I regret that
we weren't given a moment
before take-off to shake hands,
trade names, maybe pray
like members of an expedition
traveling a territory both visible
and not visible, both deadly
and kind. The kid to my left

is in the "Navy Police." Though,
with his baby-face, he'd do better
in a powder-blue tuxedo enlisting
a purple corsage for the prom.
Across the aisle a businessman
taps his brass ring on the tray,
and when the wings shudder

his wife just keeps her eyes closed,
and the redhead who needlepoints
never even glances at the gigantic
blackness –   which must be
exactly what the pilots see, what
a bug sees when something
hungry suddenly swallows it whole.

We could easily be lost in the great
gulp of the ultimate toad,
but only a bug-eyed child is crying.
We could be a single mile
from the side of a mountain
that would make us *the extra*
to read all about, and I just want
somebody to tell me how
to keep on living these hours
completely blind to what's ahead.

And I am black; the wig-wearing
woman is white, the navy kid
is Filipino – and we're way, way
above America, riding a machine
none of us can explain, believing
the future has reserved a seat
for us, so why *aren't* we a little
more willing to see each other
in light of all the nighttime
that surrounds us?

I spend a lot of darkness
trying not to give up
on being human, listening
to the engines of powerful things
moving us around: the war
makers, the iron maiden
of capital, the fundamentalists
sharpening their one crooked
stick, television – the imperceptible
swarm filling the air,

and how can I *not* say
this jet   is like the world?
All umpteen-trillion tons
of impossible Earth
zooming along
near the speed of sound,
carrying so many people
thinking about something else.

First Verse

I admit the world remains almost beautiful.
The dung beetles snap on their iridescent jackets
despite the canine holiness of the Vatican
and, despite the great predatory surge of industry,
two human hands still mate like butterflies
when buttoning a shirt.
                              Some mornings
I take myself away from the television
and go outside where the only news comes
as fresh air folding over the houses.
And I feel glad for an hour in which race
and power and all the momentum of history
add up to nothing.

As if from all the mad grinding
in my brain, a single blue lily had grown –
my skull open like a lake. I can hear
an insect   sawing itself into what must be
a kind of speech.
                              I know there is little
mercy to be found among us, that we have
already agreed to go down fighting, but
I should be more amazed: look
at the blood   and guess who's holding
the knives. Shouldn't we be *more
amazed?* Doesn't the view
just blister your eyes?

To have come this long way, to stand
on two legs, to be   not tarantulas
or chimpanzees   but soldiers of our own
dim-witted enslavement. To utterly miss the door
to the enchanted palace. To see *myself*
coined into a stutter. To allow the money

to brand us   and the believers
to blindfold our lives.
                    In the name
of what? If that old book was true
the first verse would say *Embrace*

the world. Be friendly. The forests
are glad you breathe.

I see now
the Earth itself *does*   have a face.
If it could say *I*   it would
plead with the universe, the way
dinosaurs once growled
at the stars.
                    It's like
the road behind us is stolen
completely   so the future can
never arrive.   So, look at this: look
what we've *done*. With all
we knew.
With all we knew
that we knew.

Really Breathing

after Pablo Neruda

*You are confined but not alone. Many are the
prisoners who walk the open streets.*

— Jesus

I am tortured by smoke
from cigarettes, by the stink
of industry   and by certain
sparrows, their wary glances –
as if my crumbs were
a kind of tarot, as if in each
tiny crunch   they could read my life.

It just so happens that I am sick
of being Black. And it also happens
that I stumble into gymnasiums
and shopping malls dying secretly
like a centipede in a teacup, like one
bullfrog harrumping his bass throb
for an audience of rubber ducks.

I see one man kiss another
and my pulse applauds
the cozy sombrero under which
they samba, but of course,
my country goes back
to the goose-step, scrapes the sun
from the sky – then the faces
are bloody and hatred licks
its blessèd fists. Why even
mention it?

I am sick of being measured
by the nappiness of my head.
And sick of imagining myself

from other points of view. I am
sick of thoughts   especially
thoughts about race. I think
maybe the world is also
unwell   or it could be my
attitude: hostile, yet
compassionate with a pinch
of sincere disappointment.

Maybe the only thing I need
is a woman with crow-black hair
tangled between her legs. Ahhh, to be
made deaf by the blaze of her thighs
tied around my head, to be that
perfectly blind. What holy music
would find me then?

If I could I would speak only Xhosa
and sing songs with Mandela.
I would spin my brain
into a Spanish encyclopedia
and trade bluesy pentameters
with brother Pablo. I want
to turn my soul all the way up
and play Hendrix until the quiet
African nuns sling their habits
back to Europe and teach
the roseate labyrinth of their labia,
the foliage of the first theology.

It continues to be true that race
sickens me. I have not forgotten
where this started. Race wants
to make each of us a beetle

on a string – especially *Whiteness*
that insinuates itself as capital,
that imagines itself indispensable,
that spoons itself to everyone
as medicine for its own psychosis.

Still, it would be rather hip
to meet Annabella Sciorra, to invite her
delicious Italian lips over
for a little Caesar salad, to see her
smile at some lonely sandwich
I've kissed with paprika   or maybe
she's obsessed with the friendly leaves
of cilantro   or she and I could grab
some piccolos and blow Sun Ra
until we jangled into banjos. Hey,
just because The Monster
holds you in its mouth,
don't believe everything isn't
willing to happen. *Everything is!*

I believe it shall be
more than reasonable, in fact,
to roller-blade around the downtowns
brandishing a clumsy erection –
big as a plantain – to hurl it
like a boomerang at Halliburton
and Exxon and the others whose
long corporate fangs staple our necks,
to make our world much too gooey
for Mr. and Mrs. Dow Jones.

Don't get me wrong. I know
this *is* America, and I'm glad

to wake up in the womanly arms
of gravity, to feel the Earth still
unready to give me up, but
wouldn't it be a lovely day, the day
when people bleeding in factories
went home for good with their lives
in their own good hands?

I just don't want so many
broken bones in our bones. Am I
crazy? Who really *wants* an economy
based on suffering? That we go on
like this   is merely proof that
evil wears some really sexy clothes.

I can't go on being Mr. Middle Class.
I can't keep staring at a menu
while somebody's chewing
my face. You can't assign me
a color   without wondering
if I'm actually   a man. *Am I*
a man? Is slavery
over? Look around. You
cannot set up this much
damage and not drop
a log of shit right
in the middle of your
own bright plate, right
between that *other*
white meat and the mashed
potatoes.

So, here we are: new stadiums,
beauty shops, the big-ass houses,

the gun-sucking cops, and always the fat
American cars and people who ask
nothing dangerous. . . . How did
our tax money, for example, inspire
the Bush bombing of Baghdad
rather than prodigious groves
of cannabis tended lovingly
by the National Guard?

Everywhere fresh prisons and bottom
lines: terrible jobs, terrible
choices, terrible. Look at the flies
dead, so close to freedom –
the window smiling,
the glass sweet as a guillotine.
If you feel no kinship
with the flies   well maybe
you should think a little bit
about it, maybe you should
put down your bible and
try to pick up all the blood –
maybe you should just
go fuck yourself.

I am sick enough to walk
like the great feathered snake,
to ghost dance all over
my country, to throw up
a galaxy   of better worlds.
That's why when the Christians
see me coming   the day tears
like a perineum amidst a titanic
birth and Jesus runs to every
cathedral and church screaming

No! No! No! with his dark
Palestinian eyes flared
like the barrels of a shotgun. Friday
I saw him
with a weed-eater
chasing the Reverend Jerry Falwell:
Zzssst – Zzssst – Zzssst on his sorry ass.

Jesus is sick of being black too.
And of the notion of sin
and of so many gazillions hanging
onto his wounds. He told me
two times, "Tim, HEAVEN
is HERE! You gutless
termite," but twice
I forgave him   despite my
chronic rage. He wore his skin
like a favorite shirt, like a roaming
storm. Of course, to varying degrees,
I am undone by American history.

I am. Truly.
That's why when I
speak up – my heart like a
switchblade, my buffalo head
bristling with English – I feel
my lungs start to keel over
right down to my knees, and even
the everywhere animal of air
turns its back on me. But,
but   who's
really breathing   anyway?

Appendix

Aditi: Hindu, Mother Goddess of all heavenly bodies, deities, plants, and animals (India)

AIM: American Indian Movement

Annabella Sciorra: movie actress, first known for her role as the controversial love interest of "Flipper" (Wesley Snipes) in the movie *Jungle Fever*

belightedly: invented word meaning full of light

The Chi-Lites: a R&B vocal group that came to prominence in the '60s

The Dells: another R&B vocal group of the same era

Es todo, ese: Chicano slang meaning *that's all man* or *I'm it, bro*

flaze: invented word meaning blinding fire

flubber: a make-believe rubber-like substance with fantastic elasticity and spring (Disney)

Fannie Lou Hamer: civil rights activist, Field Secretary of the Student Nonviolent Coordinating Committee ('60s)

Haumea: Mother Goddess of love and sexuality (Hawai'i)

hooptee: old, beat-up car

Moombi: Creator of the Earth, She who blesses the seeds (Kenya)

Morpheus: radical/cyber-terrorist from the movie *The Matrix*

P-funk: *pure funk*, a style of music developed by composer George Clinton and his band, Parliament Funkadelic

Pippen: Scottie Pippen of the 6-time NBA Champion Chicago Bulls

plovers: birds that feed along the ocean shore

Sade: Sade Adu, R&B vocalist

semper fi: always faithful (an expression often associated with the U.S. Marines)

yockin': black slang (circa. Philadelphia, late '60s, early '70s) a verb meaning to dress lavishly in loud colors, derivative of the noun *yockimo*, also slang